Improving Reading Comprehension
Grade 4

Table of Contents

Improving Reading Comprehension
Grade 4
Introduction

Introduction

We have all watched a child struggle while learning to read. Each new word can be a challenge or a frustration. We have joined in the child's struggle, teaching the skills needed to decode unfamiliar words and make sense of the letters. Then we have experienced joy as the child mastered the words and began to read sentences, gaining confidence with each new success.

Learning to read is one of the most important skills students ever acquire. By the fourth grade, most children are independent, confident readers. The emphasis now can be placed on practicing the valuable skills of reading comprehension. When a child reads without understanding, he or she will quickly become disinterested. Readers need to develop the skill of making sense of new words through context. They need to understand an author's message, whether stated or implied. They need to see how each event in a story affects the rest of the story and its characters. These are all important skills that must be nurtured if a student is to be a successful reader. Reading comprehension is vital throughout the curriculum in school and for success in many other areas of life.

To build the necessary skills for reading comprehension, a reading program should clear away other stresses so that the student can concentrate on the reading. With that in mind, the stories in *Improving Reading Comprehension* have been written to interest and engage the readers. They are short to hold the reader's attention. The exercises are short but effective tools to determine the student's understanding of each story. Given as homework or class work, the two-page assignments can easily be incorporated into existing reading programs for practice and reinforcement of reading comprehension skills.

Organization

The stories in *Improving Reading Comprehension* have been divided into six chapters: School Days, On the Move, Family Ties, You Never Know..., All About Animals, and Mystery and Adventure. The stories are a mix of fantasy, nonfiction, and realistic fiction.

Each story includes one or two comprehension exercises. These exercises concentrate on the student's understanding of the story. Many exercises emphasize vocabulary as well. The exercises include completing sentences, matching words with definitions, labeling, finding words with similar meanings, multiple-choice questions, cloze, and crossword puzzles. Each story and its exercise are complete on two sides of one tear-out sheet.

The Curriculum Correlation chart on Page 4 will allow you to include the reading in other curriculum areas.

There is a Letter to Parents on Page 5, and a Letter to Students is on Page 6. Notifying students and parents of a new activity beforehand will help answer students' questions and keep parents informed.

There are four assessments. Each assessment can be used individually or paired with another, and in any order.

Use

Improving Reading Comprehension is designed for independent use by students. Copies of the stories and activities can be given to individual students, pairs of students, or small groups for completion. They can also be used as a center activity.

To begin, determine the implementation that fits your students' needs and your classroom structure. The following plan suggests a format for this implementation.

1. **Explain** the purpose of the activities to your class.

2. **Review** the mechanics of how you want students to work with the exercises. You may wish to introduce the subject of each article. You may decide to tap into students' prior knowledge of the subject for discussion. You might plan a group discussion after the reading.

3. **Remind** students that they are reading for understanding. Tell them to read carefully. Remind them to use a dictionary when necessary if the context is not enough to help them figure out a word.

4. **Determine** how you will monitor the Assessments. Each assessment is designed to be used independently. You may decide to administer the assessments to the whole class, to small groups that have completed a unit, or to individuals as they work through the book. The assessments can be used as pre- and post-evaluations of the students' progress.

Additional Notes

1. **Parent Communication.** Use the Letter to Parents, and encourage the students to share the Letter to Students with their parents. Decide if you want to keep the activity pages and assessments in portfolios for conferencing, or if you want students to take them home as they are completed.

2. **Bulletin Boards.** Since a key to comprehension is discussion, encourage students to illustrate, add to, or do further research on their favorite stories. Display the students' work on a bulletin board.

3. **Have Fun.** Reading should be fun, and the stories in *Improving Reading Comprehension* will capture students' interest and stimulate their imagination. Fun group discussions, ideas, or games that evolve from the reading will enhance the learning experience.

Improving Reading Comprehension
Grade 4

Curriculum Correlation

Story Title	Social Studies	Language Arts	Science	Math	Physical Education
Putting It Off		X			
Making the Grade		X			
Birds of a Feather	X	X			
Dream Team	X	X			X
Class Country	X	X			
Can Do!		X		X	
Back to School	X	X			
Dreaming of Sleep		X			
Friends Forever	X	X			
Going Places	X	X			
Far from Home	X	X			
A Train in Spain	X	X			
Space Place		X	X		
Night Lights	X	X			
Lunch Lessons	X	X			
Families	X	X			
Too Hot or Not?	X	X	X		
The Museum		X			
The Best Present	X	X			
City Summer	X	X			
Memorial Day	X	X			
Enough Gloves	X	X			
Play Ball!	X	X			X
Sylvia's Bear	X	X			
Mystery House	X	X			
Spilled Milk		X			
Chili Surprise!	X	X			
Hats Off!	X	X			
Good Guy	X	X			
Animals in Space		X	X		
Scaredy Cat		X			
Bedelia		X			
Not a Word Bird		X			
A Cat for Company		X			
Animal Show		X			
Stranded	X	X			X
Ghostly Towns	X	X			
Castles		X	X		
See Monsters?		X	X		
A New View	X	X			
Movie Mystery		X			
The Trunk		X			

Dear Parents:

Learning to read is clearly one of the most important things your child will ever do. By the fourth grade, most children are confident, independent readers. They have developed a large vocabulary and have learned ways to understand the meanings of some unfamiliar words through context.

What is equally important for all readers, however, is reading with understanding. If your child reads a story but is unable to describe the events in his or her own words or answer questions about the story, then the reading loses its meaning. Young readers need practice to strengthen their reading comprehension abilities.

With this goal in mind, our class will be working with a book of stories and activities that will reinforce reading comprehension. The short stories are a mix of fiction and nonfiction. The stories are fun, and the one-page exercises are varied. Without feeling the pressure of a long story to remember or many pages of exercises to work, your child will develop a better understanding of the reading and have fun doing it!

Occasionally, your child may bring home an activity. Please consider the following suggestions to help your child work successfully.

- Provide a quiet place to work.
- If your child is reading, help to find the meanings of difficult words through the context of the story. Discuss the story.
- Go over the directions for the exercises together.
- Check the lesson when it is complete. Note areas of improvement as well as concern.

Thank you for being involved with your child's learning. A strong reading foundation will lead to a lifetime of reading enjoyment and success.

Cordially,

Dear Student:

Do you like to read? You can probably remember your favorite book. You could probably tell a friend what happened in the story. Maybe you talked to someone in your family about it.

It is good to think and talk about what you read. This can help you to remember and to understand what you read.

We will be working with a book of short stories. After reading each one, you will be asked to think about the story. Then you will answer some questions. Thinking about these stories will help you practice for reading longer stories and help you become a better reader.

The stories are a mix of facts and fun. There are animal stories and stories of school. There are stories about people on the move. You will read mystery and adventure stories. Read carefully and have fun. There is a story here for everyone!

Sincerely,

Assessment 1

Directions

Read the paragraphs. Then choose the best word to complete each sentence. Write the word on the line.

The kennel sold poodle and collie pups, and as Bobby walked down the aisle between the pens with the beautiful pups, he wanted them all. The dogs yipped and came to the screen to lick his fingers. Bobby said that picking one dog would be like freeing it, but the man who sold the dogs said, "All of these pups will find homes. Today, people want pure-blooded dogs."

Bobby's father suggested that they look at other dogs before Bobby made his choice, so they visited other kennels. Bobby saw so many kinds of dogs that he felt confused. The last stop had a sign reading "County Humane Society."

1. Bobby said picking one dog would be like _____ it.
   feeling   freeing   taking

2. The man said people wanted pure-_____ dogs.
   boned   colored   blooded

3. Bobby's father _____ they look at other dogs.
   suggested   sampled   while

4. Bobby saw so many dogs he felt _____.
   cornered   sick   confused

5. The last stop was the _____ Society.
   Human   Howling   Humane

Assessment 2

Directions

Read the paragraphs. Choose a word from the paragraphs with the same meaning as the underlined words. Write the word on the line.

Consider for a moment how different your life might be if you had to walk to get wherever you needed to go. Of course, everyone else would be walking, too! Anything you needed to carry would be on your back or on your head. This would have been the way to travel had you lived 7,000 years ago.

Now let's make things a little easier. You may imagine that you have a horse or a donkey to ride. These will get you where you want to go much more quickly. But remember to watch out for the weather, because your horse will not protect you from rain, and it has no heater to keep you warm if it snows! You also need to consider that the roads are far from the smooth, tarred avenues to which you have become accustomed. These roads, when there are roads, are rough and rutted dirt and rocks. And when it rains, they are mud!

1. <u>Think about</u> how different your life would be if you had to walk everywhere you went. _____

2. Now <u>pretend</u> that you have a horse or donkey to ride. _____

3. Your horse will not <u>keep you safe</u> from rain or snow. _____

4. You will not be traveling on the smooth <u>roads</u> that we have today.

   _____

5. The roads are rough and <u>full of deep track marks</u>. _____

Assessment 3

Directions

Read the paragraphs. Then answer the questions about the story. Circle the letter in front of the correct answer.

Arthur wanted to come to the class party as a fierce and beautiful bird. Most of the fierce and beautiful birds were already taken. He was considering coming as a blue jay. Bruce said that blue jays are mean and sassy but not fierce.

"Why don't you come as a whooping crane?" Peter said. "Whooping cranes are nearly extinct, so you wouldn't even have to show up." Willa was coming as a dove, so she felt it was her job to make peace. "I have an idea," she whispered to Arthur.

1. What kind of bird did Arthur want to be?
   a. wild and colorful
   b. fierce and beautiful
   c. quiet and bright

2. Peter said Arthur should come as a whooping crane because _____.
   a. they are almost extinct
   b. they are fierce and beautiful
   c. it was the only bird left

3. Willa is probably going to _____.
   a. make Arthur feel embarrassed
   b. let Arthur be the dove
   c. help Arthur with her idea

Assessment 4

Directions

Read the paragraph. Then choose a word from the paragraph that fits each clue. Write the words in the puzzle.

Ghost towns exist for several reasons. One of the most common is changes in economics. Many ghost towns started out as busy mill towns or quarry towns. People came to the town to work in the mill or quarry. Then people came who set up bakeries, schools, and shops. Soon, there was a community. But perhaps the resource was used up. Or someone found a better stone to use. Then people stopped buying the product that kept the town going. Soon people began to move away to look for other work. When there were not enough people to support the small businesses, they too closed. Eventually, the town became deserted. Many of the towns that began in the west when people searched for gold were left when there was no gold to be found, or the mines were emptied.

ACROSS:
3. in time
4. the making and managing of goods and services
5. a mine

DOWN:
1. something that is a source of wealth
2. something produced

Putting It Off

"John," Miss Archer said in her strong voice, "you're a terrible procrastinator!" John's face turned red, but he was more upset than embarrassed. "You haven't picked out a book to read yet."

"How could she call me something like that?" he thought. "And she said it right in front of the whole class." He wasn't sure what a procrastinator was, but it didn't sound very nice. He was certain that he was not one of those, whatever it was.

"Did you hear what she called me?" John asked Melissa after school. "I feel like telling my mother. Can I use a word like that in front of my mother?"

"Well," Melissa sighed, "she said you are a terrible procrastinator. I suppose that's better than being good at it. Why don't you look the word up in the dictionary tonight and find out?"

The next day Melissa asked John if he had looked up the word *procrastinator*. "No," John said. "I was going to, but I didn't get around to it. I'll look it up later today."

"Well, I looked it up," Melissa said. "It means a person who always puts things off instead of doing them now."

"Oh," John said. "Well, I'll worry about it some other time."

Go on to next page.

Directions

Answer each question about the story. Circle the letter in front of the correct answer.

1. John thinks that the word Miss Archer calls him is _____.
   a. a way of saying he is a good student
   b. not a very nice sounding word
   c. her way of getting him to use a dictionary
   d. a name for a person who reads fast

2. John is embarrassed because Miss Archer talks about him _____.
   a. to John's mother
   b. behind his back
   c. to the whole class
   d. over a loudspeaker

3. At first Melissa thinks that by calling John a "terrible procrastinator," Miss Archer means that he is _____.
   a. not good at procrastinating
   b. her favorite student
   c. a very careful reader
   d. very good at procrastinating

4. Miss Archer is saying that John _____.
   a. does not know how to read
   b. loses his temper easily
   c. always runs to his mother
   d. always puts things off

5. In the end, John proves that Miss Archer is _____.
   a. right about his being a procrastinator
   b. unfair to call him a procrastinator
   c. trying to say something nice about him
   d. sorry she says what she does to the whole class

Making the Grade

"Donna, have you done all your homework?" asked her father.

"Yes, Dad," said Donna. All except for her project, that is. Donna had a big project due the next week. She was doing a report on a famous American. She had chosen to report on the artist, Georgia O'Keeffe. Other than choosing her subject, Donna had not done much work on her project yet. After all, she had until the next week.

Donna felt bored. She called her friend, Trish. Trish was at the library doing research for her project. Then she called Sarah, but Sarah was out taking photographs for her project. Donna decided she might as well work on her own project. She began looking through her parents' collection of books for information. Then she got on the computer and looked for more information. She found pictures of the artist and her paintings. She began to organize her information. It felt good to be getting ahead on her work.

The next day, Donna went to the library to do her own research. Then she bought a large piece of poster board and tried different arrangements of her pictures and information. For several days, Donna worked hard. She found that Georgia O'Keeffe was an interesting woman. Donna was enjoying herself. When she finished her project with a day to spare, she was proud of her achievement. Her parents were pleased with the way she had worked, too. They had always told her not to wait until the last minute. Now she thought she knew why.

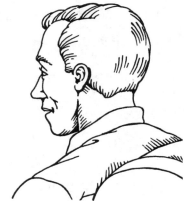

Donna gave her presentation and got an A. Her teacher said it was obvious that she had put much effort into it. Donna was very happy. She couldn't wait to tell her parents about the A she had earned!

Go on to next page.

Directions

Think about the passage you read. Then fill in the blanks of the following paragraph with words from the Word List.

Word List

organize   spare   achievement   obvious
American   presentation   arrangements   research

Donna had to do a project on a famous **1)** _____.

She usually waited until the last minute to do her work, but she was

bored. She went to the library to **2)** _____ her

project. She began to **3)** _____ her information.

She tried out different **4)** _____ of her work on a

piece of poster board. She finished her work with a day to **5)** _____.

Donna gave her **6)** _____. Her teacher said it was

7) _____ that she had put much effort into her project. She was

proud of her **8)** _____.

Use the Word List above to choose the correct word for each meaning. Write your choice on the line.

9. a citizen of America _____

10. easy to see _____

11. to put in order _____

12. something done with great effort _____

13. left over, extra _____

14. careful study of a subject _____

15. things set in a certain way _____

16. something offered to a group _____

Birds of a Feather

Everyone was planning to come to the class party as a different kind of bird. Arthur wanted to come as some special bird that is very fierce and beautiful. Most of the fierce and beautiful birds were already taken. Bruce was coming as an eagle. Beatrice would be a falcon. Peter would be a hawk. So, Arthur had to think of something else.

Arthur was considering coming as a blue jay. Bruce said that blue jays are mean and sassy but not fierce. "Crows sound fierce sometimes," Beatrice said.

"Why don't you come as a whooping crane?" Peter said. "Whooping cranes are nearly extinct, so you wouldn't even have to show up." Willa was coming as a dove, so she felt that it was her job to make peace. "I have an idea," she whispered to Arthur.

At the party, Bruce and Peter waited to see what bird Arthur would be. Peter was teasing Bruce about looking more like a parrot than an eagle. Then Arthur came in, and everyone's eyes were on his beautiful purple and white costume. He had come as the make-believe bird, the phoenix. "In many old stories," Willa explained, "the phoenix stands for beauty, excellence, and long life."

"I wish I'd thought of that," Peter said.

Go on to next page.

Directions

Answer each question about the story. Circle the letter in front of the correct answer.

1. Which of these birds would everyone at the party think was both fierce and beautiful?
   a. a turkey
   b. a falcon
   c. a crow
   d. a whooping crane

2. Which of the children plans to be an eagle?
   a. Bruce
   b. Arthur
   c. Willa
   d. Peter

3. Peter behaves most like which kind of bird?
   a. an eagle
   b. a dove
   c. the phoenix
   d. a blue jay

4. Arthur comes to the party as which kind of bird?
   a. a blue heron
   b. a parrot
   c. the phoenix
   d. a hawk

5. Which word best tells the way Peter feels at the end of the story?
   a. jealous
   b. happy
   c. popular
   d. clever

Dream Team

John got the ball and drove it down the full length of the court. He knew he was handling the ball well. He reached the basket and put the ball up against the backboard. It went through the basket with a neat *swoosh* as John landed back on the court. A few of his Panther teammates clapped and John looked to his coach for approval, but Coach Penn was shaking his head. That was not the reaction John had expected. What was wrong?

"Everybody on the bleachers, now!" called the coach. When they had all found a seat, he studied them for a moment. "I see a good bunch of ball players here," said Coach Penn. "I also see a team that won't win a game if something doesn't change. Do you know what that is?" The boys were silent. "Teamwork!" said the coach, throwing his hands up in the air. "You have to start working together! John, you think you just made a great basket. Well, it went in the basket all right, but when you're playing a team sport, you need to act as a team. You support each other and you use each other—pass the ball, look for the open man. No player on this team stands alone; you work together, or you don't play. Now let me see some teamwork!"

The boys got back on the court. They practiced working together and passing. They had to learn to trust each other and to be there for each other. John began to look at his teammates in a different way. He began to think of the team as parts of a machine that needed to work together. He still got to the hoop and made some shots, but he only did it when it was the team's best chance to get the points.

That Friday's competition was against the Bulldogs, who had beat John's team twice last year. This time, the Panthers played the best game they had played all season. They worked together on the court like the machine John had imagined earlier in the week. The crowd screamed and cheered. It was a close game, but when the final buzzer sounded the Panthers had won, and every player had contributed to the victory. Coach Penn couldn't stop smiling. "Now *that's* the team I've been looking for!" he said.

Go on to next page.

Directions

Answer each question about the story. Circle the letter in front of the correct answer.

1. The Panthers are a _____ team.
   - **a.** golf
   - **b.** baseball
   - **c.** soccer
   - **d.** basketball

2. Coach Penn shook his head at practice because _____.
   - **a.** John missed the basket
   - **b.** the team was not playing together
   - **c.** the team was fighting
   - **d.** John was not handling the ball well

3. What is the meaning of *reaction*?
   - **a.** to do something again
   - **b.** to feel badly
   - **c.** a response to something
   - **d.** a quick movement

Write *true* or *false* next to each sentence.

4. _____ John's team is called the Bulldogs.

5. _____ The Bulldogs beat the Panthers twice last year.

6. _____ The Panthers' coach is Mr. Penn.

7. _____ Mr. Penn wanted the team to work together.

8. _____ The Panthers lost to the Bulldogs again.

Class Country

Myra's fourth-grade class had been working on a special project. They had started the day Mr. Morse came in and announced, "Today we're going to start our own country." It was part of a social studies unit on government.

At first the class didn't know how they felt about it. They thought it sounded like a lot of work. Once they began, however, they found that they were enjoying the project. They often commented that they felt as though they were charting new territory.

As the project continued, the class found that there was always something new to develop. They drew maps of their country (based on the reports of the "explorers" who returned to give them details). They outlined a system of government. Myra was in charge of developing an economic system. She had to determine how goods and services would be managed.

At the end of the project, the class was very proud of their country, even though they knew there were still problems to work out. The final work on the project included the design of a national flag, the writing of a national anthem, and the choosing of a national bird and flower. The things that sounded like hard work at the beginning of the project were becoming fun.

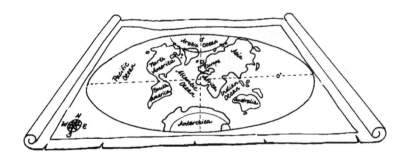

Go on to next page.

Name_____   Date_____

Directions

Answer each question about the story. Circle the letter in front of the correct answer.

1. What is Myra's class project?
   a. They are starting their own country.
   b. They are exploring new countries.
   c. They are writing a new song.
   d. They are doing a science project.

2. How did Myra's class feel about the project at first?
   a. They were excited.
   b. They were bored.
   c. They didn't know.
   d. They were angry.

3. What is an *economic system*?
   a. the way people in a country travel
   b. the way a country manages goods and services
   c. the way people make maps of countries
   d. the way people communicate

4. The class drew maps based on _____.
   a. their memory
   b. their imagination
   c. reports from "explorers"
   d. Mr. Morse's instructions

5. The final work of the project included _____.
   a. charting new territory
   b. outlining a system of government
   c. developing an economic system
   d. designing a national flag

Can Do!

Maddie and Terese pulled the wagon slowly up the hill toward Maddie's house. The wagon had grown heavy with their collection of canned foods. The people in Maddie's neighborhood had been generous with their contributions. At first, Maddie and Terese had been hesitant to knock on people's doors and ask for canned foods. Everyone was nice, however, so the girls soon felt comfortable. Some people were not at home. A few did not answer their doors. But most people donated two or three cans. This trip up the hill was the second they had made that day.

The girls were collecting the cans for a school food drive. The class that collected the most cans would get a pizza party. The cans would go to a food bank that helped people in town who needed assistance from time to time. The bank had gotten low on food and this was a way to replenish its stores. Maddie and Terese wanted their class to get the party. Between their two neighborhoods, the girls collected 135 cans. Maddie's neighborhood had more houses, so they got most of them, 78 in all, from there.

Maddie and Terese added their cans to the cans the rest of their class had collected. There were 731 cans in all. The man from the food bank was amazed with the amount of food that the students had gathered. Maddie and Terese's class won the pizza party. They enjoyed the pizza, but they also felt good knowing they had done something to help other people.

Go on to next page.

Directions

Read each clue. Choose a word from the Word List, or do the mathematical equation, to find an answer to fit each clue. Write the words in the puzzle.

Word List

replenish   generous   contributions
hesitant   donated   assistance

ACROSS:

2. gave

7. number of cans class had before Maddie and Terese added theirs (in words)

8. help

DOWN:

1. something given along with others

3. number of cans collected from Terese's neighborhood (in words)

4. willing to share

5. not certain

6. fill again

Back to School

Have you ever heard anyone say something like this? "When I was your age, I had to walk to school. It was three miles each way. We walked in all kinds of weather. It was all uphill, too!"

Much has changed in education over the years. People may exaggerate how hard things used to be. But it is true that most students of today are fortunate when compared to those of long ago. There are many places in the world today where education is still a privilege. Many children stop going to school at an early age. Families need children to work and help with expenses. Some children go to school and work, too. To them, it must seem amazing that in other countries, until the age of 16 or so, a child's only responsibility is to go to school! Even in countries like the United States, free schooling for all has only come about in the last 100 years.

Early education consisted of listening and memorizing. Students did not often get books. Paper could be scarce. Students were required to memorize and recite long lists of facts. Classrooms were very different as well. There were no centers or group projects. Students stayed in their seats. They spoke only when spoken to. Or they paid the consequences! Only very recently has education become as interesting and exciting as it is today. Teachers try to motivate students to learn. They try to show students how what they are learning relates to their own lives. Classrooms are full of color, experimentation, and fun.

Today, there is still much for students to learn. The basics are still as important as they used to be. Our changing world also makes it important for students to learn and experience much more than reading, writing, and arithmetic. School has  taken on a huge role in today's society. You may ride the bus, carpool, or walk three miles to get there. But be sure to jump in and make the most of your time at school!

Go on to next page.

Directions

Answer each question about the story. Circle the letter in front of the correct answer.

1. This story is mostly about _____.
   a. schools long ago
   b. how teachers teach
   c. what students learn
   d. how schools have changed

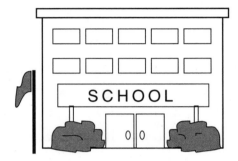

2. What is a *privilege*?
   a. a gift
   b. a lesson
   c. a special benefit
   d. a mistake

3. Students of long ago did not often have _____.
   a. discipline
   b. books
   c. teachers
   d. schools

4. How do today's teachers try to interest students?
   a. by telling jokes
   b. by comparing learning to real life
   c. by making the work easy
   d. by making them memorize

5. How might a child from another country, who has not been able to go to school, feel about coming to a school in the United States?
   a. angry
   b. disappointed
   c. afraid
   d. happy

Dreaming of Sleep

Maria was very tired after the visit to Uncle Ned's. As she rode home in the car with her mother, she could barely keep her eyes open.

"Watch out!" Maria called out all at once, sitting up straight in the seat. Maria thought she had seen Paul Bunyan's ox standing by the road, ready to cross. Before she could explain to her mother, their car had passed the ox, which was really just some big mailboxes on posts.

Maria knew that her sleepy eyes were playing tricks on her, but they fooled her again. "Oh, oh!" she sighed when she saw an ambulance stop on the road ahead of them. Then the red light turned green. It was only a traffic light and some shadows on the road.

"You certainly are jumpy tonight," Mother said. "Why don't I stop so you can get in the back seat and sleep?" When Mother stopped the car, Maria climbed into the back seat, put on her seat belt, and tried to get comfortable. She closed her weary eyes, but she couldn't get to sleep. She kept thinking that it had begun to storm. The lights from big trucks were flashing into the back seat like lightning.

"It's odd," Maria yawned, "how a person can get too tired to go to sleep anywhere but in her own bed."

Go on to next page.

Name _____   Date _____

Directions

Answer each question about the story. Circle the letter in front of the correct answer.

1. When Maria sees Paul Bunyan's ox, it turns out to be _____.
   a. a big truck parked on the side of the road
   b. a cow waiting to cross the road
   c. some big mailboxes on posts
   d. some shadows on the road

2. Maria thinks that a traffic light is _____.
   a. an ambulance
   b. the eyes of a big ox
   c. the back of a truck
   d. lightning

3. In the back seat, Maria cannot sleep because of _____.
   a. a bad dream
   b. a storm
   c. her mother's voice
   d. lights from trucks

4. Maria is seeing things that are not there because she is _____.
   a. tired and can't sleep
   b. not at all sleepy
   c. trying to read in the car
   d. having a dream

5. At the end of the story, Maria feels certain that she will be able to sleep when _____.
   a. they turn onto a different road
   b. they finally get home
   c. she gets tired enough
   d. she gives up and closes her eyes

Friends Forever

After Kristin and her mom had moved to Maine from the town in Florida where they had always lived, she missed her friend, Nicky. Kristin and Nicky had promised to write to each other, but neither girl was sure that they would stick to their agreement.

After a year, though, they were still writing faithfully. In each letter, Nicky told Kristin news about the people and places in the town where they had both grown up. Kristin enjoyed her new home, but reading Nicky's letters made her think longingly of familiar people and places.

Kristin's letters to Nicky were quite different. They told about exciting new experiences. They told of snow, sleds, skis, snowmobiles, and other winter things that were new to Kristin. Reading Kristin's letters made Nicky want to visit her badly.

Kristin surprised Nicky with a phone call one day to tell her about an idea that her mother had. She invited Nicky to visit her new home during winter vacation. She also asked if Nicky's family would let her stay with them for a few weeks in the summer.

Nicky asked her parents about Kristin's suggestion. They said it would be fine, but they wanted her to help pay for her trip by earning some of the money herself. Nicky agreed, but when she sat down to figure out her plans, she was unable to think of any ideas to finance her trip. She wrote to Kristin asking for ideas.

Go on to next page.

Name_____   Date_____

Directions

Rewrite each sentence. Use a word with the same meaning from the Word List in place of the underlined words.

Word List
skis   finance   faithfully   unable
longingly   suggestion   agreement   snowmobiles

1. Kristin and Nicky wrote to each other <u>loyally</u> for a year.

_____

2. Kristin thought <u>with longing</u> about her old town.

_____

3. Nicky asked her parents about the <u>idea put forth</u> by Kristin's mother.

_____

4. Nicky's parents wanted her to help <u>pay for</u> the trip.

_____

5. Nicky asked Kristin for ideas about ways to earn money when she was <u>not able</u> to think of any on her own.

_____

_____

Use words from the Word List above to label the pictures.

_____   _____   _____

Going Places

Consider for a moment how different your life might be if you had to walk to get wherever you needed to go. Of course, everyone else would be walking, too! Anything you needed to carry would be on your back or on your head. This would have been the way to travel had you lived 7,000 years ago.

Now let's make things a little easier. You may imagine that you have a horse or a donkey to ride. These will get you where you want to go much more quickly. But remember to watch out for the weather, because your horse will not protect you from rain, and it has no heater to keep you warm if it snows! You also need to consider that the roads are far from the smooth, tarred avenues to which you have become accustomed. These roads, when there are roads, are rough and rutted dirt and rocks. And when it rains, they are mud!

Let's say that you have invented a carriage or a wagon of sorts now, so you can travel in style. If you are a passenger, you have a place to sit out of the weather. As the driver, however, you will still have to contend with the cold and rain. The roads have improved very little. Trips still require much planning because the travel is not very fast—especially by today's standards!

Hold on to your hat. We are going to move full speed ahead to today. Now you can go anywhere in the world in less than a day. You have soft seats to sit in, cup holders for your drinks, and windows to let in just the amount of weather you want. You can even listen to music as you travel. You can drive, sail, or fly in comfort—or if you want to, you can still walk!

Go on to next page.

29

Directions

Answer each question about the story. Circle the letter in front of the correct answer.

1. What is this story mostly about?
   a. horses and donkeys
   b. modern travel
   c. travel through the years
   d. boats of long ago

2. What is the meaning of the phrase, *to which you have become accustomed*?
   a. the way you have been dressed
   b. what you have become used to
   c. what you think is correct
   d. the way you like to do things

3. A carriage would not protect you from weather unless _____.
   a. you were the driver
   b. you were pulling it
   c. you were a passenger
   d. you rolled up the windows

4. One reason travel was rougher years ago is that _____.
   a. the roads were very rough
   b. people did not know how to drive
   c. the horses did not know where to go
   d. everything was very far away

5. If you used only horses for travel, the biggest change in your life would most likely be _____.
   a. you would not go to school
   b. you would not have friends
   c. you would live in a different place
   d. you would not travel as far or as often

Far from Home

Laot Si's father taught at the university. When he came home to tell his family that they would live in the United States for a year while he taught at an American university, Laot Si looked dismayed. "What is wrong?" asked her father. "It will be most educational to visit another country, especially one that is so different from our own. You speak English very well, so you should have little trouble getting to know the people."

"I know, Papa, but it is such a large country, and what I know about the culture— the noise, the fast way of life, the cars—it seems frightening to me."

"It is not all like what you hear about or read about. I know that you will make many friends, and you will be grateful for the experience your whole life." Laot Si's father was not really confident about this, but he knew he should go. He wanted his family to be happy about the adventure, too.

They had not been in their new home very long, and a family from the university invited them to dinner. The daughter of the family was about Laot Si's age, and their fathers thought they might enjoy getting to know one another. They were both bashful at first, but soon the American girl, Jenny, was telling her new friend all about her school and friends. She asked all about Laot Si's country.

When the evening was over, their fathers asked the girls if they had enjoyed becoming acquainted. Jenny and Laot Si both laughed, a little embarrassed at being questioned in that way. Finally, Jenny offered, "I think we could probably write a book about how different our countries are."

"And," added Laot Si, "about how much alike they are, too." The girls smiled at each other because they knew they had made a friendship that would mean a great deal to each of them.

Go on to next page.

Name _____   Date _____

Directions

Read each sentence. Choose a word from the Word List that has the same meaning as the word or words in bold print. Write the word on the line.

Word List
culture   confident   educational
acquainted   bashful   dismayed

1. Laot Si's father said the year in America would be **something that would teach**.

_____

2. He was not **sure** that the family would enjoy their experience. _____

3. Laot Si was **made full of concern** by her father's news. _____

4. Laot Si and Jenny were **shy** at first. _____

5. They told each other about their own **country's ways**. _____

6. They were glad they had gotten **to know each other**. _____

Write *true* or *false* next to each sentence.

7. _____ Laot Si did not want to go to America.

8. _____ Laot Si's father taught at a university.

9. _____ Laot Si went to Jenny's house for lunch.

10. _____ Jenny taught at a university in America.

11. _____ Jenny and Laot Si became friends.

12. _____ Jenny went to Laot Si's country to visit.

A Train in Spain

Alex and his father went by jet to Spain. When they got there, they decided to travel on the train, which most people take to get from one town to another. Alex wanted to meet the people.

The train was nearly empty when Alex and his father boarded to go 100 kilometers to the next big city. There were many empty wooden seats.

The train creaked along very slowly, stopping at every little town. More and more people got on board. It was Sunday, and Alex could hear the excited voices of people crowding the platform near the tracks as the train approached each station.

The passengers carried small children, wicker luggage, baskets of food, and even some live chickens. People soon filled all the aisles, and some had to climb in and out of the train's open windows when it came to their stations.

Everyone was very friendly. People shared their lunches with Alex and his father, who joined in singing jolly songs. Alex had to shout to answer many questions about America. The trip took over six hours, and it was a hoarse and tired boy who bid good-bye to all his new friends.

"That was a wonderful trip," Alex told his father, "and I want to travel with the people of Spain again before we leave. But let's rent a car for a while."

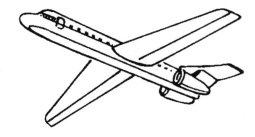

Go on to next page.

Directions

Answer each question about the story. Circle the letter in front of the correct answer.

1. The most important part of Alex's trip on the train is the chance to _____.
   a. meet the people of Spain
   b. get a free lunch
   c. hurry to another city
   d. see live chickens

2. A good word to describe the train during most of the trip is _____.
   a. *fast*
   b. *comfortable*
   c. *crowded*
   d. *quiet*

3. The people on the train are very _____.
   a. selfish
   b. generous
   c. impatient
   d. private

4. Alex becomes hoarse because _____.
   a. the train's windows are open
   b. he is calling out the name of each town
   c. he has to shout to keep his seat
   d. he sings and answers many questions

5. Alex wants to rent a car because _____.
   a. he does not enjoy the trip by train
   b. he wants to meet more people
   c. the train ride makes him very tired
   d. the train ride is too scary

Space Place

Imagine that you and your family are moving to a space station for a year. How will your life be different than it is today? What kinds of changes can you expect? Astronauts have lived in space stations. They, and the scientists who study them, can answer these questions.

You may have already guessed one huge difference between living on Earth and living in a space station. Gravity is the force that holds us to Earth. There is no gravity in a space station. This is known as *zero G*. Astronauts have to adapt to zero G. They learn how to move around. They do this by gently pushing themselves in the direction they wish to go. Zero G has other effects on the body. The heart does not have to work as hard. It becomes smaller. People's legs become slightly smaller, too. Astronauts need to feel the pull of gravity occasionally. They need to get used to it again before coming back to Earth. Scientists have developed special equipment to help astronauts deal with this.

Sleeping in space is very comfortable. It has been described by one astronaut as the "world's best waterbed." But while they sleep, the astronauts' arms float out in front of them!

There is a feeling of separation in space. The astronauts can feel cut off from Earth. To make them feel more "at home," scientists have recommended lights that imitate day and night.

Astronauts in a space station wear regular clothing when they are inside. All their clothing is designed not to burn. When they leave the station, astronauts wear special gear. They must be protected from space and the sun. These suits are quite heavy. Together with the oxygen tanks and other equipment, they can weigh as much as 180 pounds! In space, however, the suits do not feel heavy. The astronauts can move quite well.

You and your family could expect to deal with all the same things that the astronauts do. Do you think you would like to live in space?

Go on to next page.

Name_____   Date_____

Directions

Read each clue. Choose a word from the Word List that fits each clue. Write the words in the puzzle.

Word List
gravity   zero G   astronauts   adapt
effects   separation   recommended   imitate

ACROSS:

3. what one should do
4. space travelers
5. get used to
8. act like someone or
   something else

DOWN:

1. results
2. keeping apart
6. force that holds
   things together
7. having none of #6

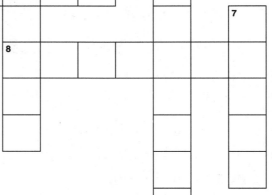

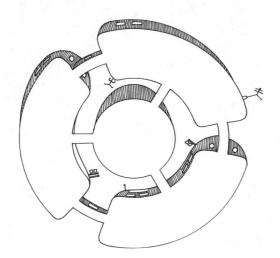

Night Lights

Betty's family moved into the house by the highway in the fall. The back of the house looked out over a little meadow between the house and a woods. Its trees grew on a steep hill that ran down to a creek. On the other side of the creek was another hill.

Betty became very interested in the lights she could see from a house on the far hill. At night it had many shining windows. As the leaves fell off the trees, she could see more of it; but she could not tell much about it. "It must be very grand," she thought. "It must be a much bigger house than our new home. I wonder who lives in such a grand house."

One evening Betty and her father got in the car and found the narrow road the other house was on. They had trouble deciding which house was the one Betty had seen. "None of the houses on this road looks so special up close," she said. Then all at once, she said, "This is the house. I know because I can see our house across the valley. But ours looks bigger from here."

The sun was setting, and it reflected off the windows of Betty's new house. "Look!" she cried. "Our house has golden windows!" On the way home she thought about the people who lived in the house she had seen. "They must look over at us and wonder who lives in the special house with the golden windows," she thought.

Go on to next page.

Directions

Answer each question about the story. Circle the letter in front of the correct answer.

1. The house that Betty sees sits _____.
   a. on a busy highway
   b. at the edge of the woods behind her house
   c. on a hill on the other side of a creek
   d. in the middle of a meadow

2. Before she sees it up close, the house Betty looks at seems _____.
   a. much grander than her new house
   b. not very special at all
   c. a lot like the house she lived in
   d. dark and gloomy

3. When they drive to find it, Betty finally knows the house she watched because _____.
   a. it is so special and grand
   b. it has very special windows
   c. she can see her house across the valley
   d. very special people are living in it

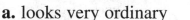

4. From across the valley, Betty's house _____.
   a. looks very ordinary
   b. has golden windows
   c. is difficult to see
   d. looks very small

5. When Betty gets back to her new house, she probably thinks that it is _____.
   a. not grand at all
   b. too far from the house she watched
   c. on the wrong side of the creek
   d. a very special place to live

Unit II: On the Move

Lunch Lessons

Mother wouldn't be back until three o'clock and had left lunch in the refrigerator. It was up to the children to put out the meal and clean up afterwards.

"You're the girl," Pedro said to Rosa, "so you can put the lunch on the table *and* clean up after we eat."

"I would have done both," Rosa said, "because you are my dear brothers. But since you put it that way, you put out the food, and I'll clean up." Soon Pedro was hungry enough to get out the sandwiches and warm the soup in the microwave oven.

Juanito wanted a pickle, and Pedro found a new jar. Its lid was stuck on very tight, and both Pedro and Juanito tried with all their might to twist it off. "It just won't budge, Juanito," Pedro said. "We'll have to go without pickles."

"Want me to try to open it?" Rosa asked.

"You can't," Pedro snorted. "Even if you weren't a girl, you couldn't open it."

"If I can open it, will you clean up after lunch?" Rosa asked. Pedro agreed. Rosa turned away from the boys and then turned right back with the lid in one hand and the opened jar in the other.

"Amazing!" Pedro cried. "How did you do that?"

"That was easy," Rosa said, picking up a spoon on the counter behind her. "I just read the label. It says, 'Tap lid with a spoon before trying to open.' "

Go on to next page.

Directions ————————————————————————

Answer each question about the story. Circle the letter in front of the correct answer.

1. Pedro says that Rosa should do all the work because _____.
   a. Rosa is the oldest
   b. Mother said that she should
   c. he makes the sandwiches
   d. Rosa is a girl

2. Rosa says that Pedro must do his share of the work because he _____.
   a. acts as if it is girls' work
   b. is hungry and she is not
   c. is the oldest child
   d. knows where to find the pickles

3. Pedro thinks Rosa cannot open the jar because _____.
   a. the lid on the jar is broken
   b. she does not know where the pickles are
   c. he thinks a girl is not strong enough
   d. Mother did not say they could have pickles

4. After lunch, the kitchen is cleaned by _____.
   a. Mother
   b. Juanito
   c. Pedro
   d. Rosa

5. Rosa is able to open the jar because she _____.
   a. finds a magic spoon
   b. reads the directions
   c. really wants a pickle
   d. is stronger than Pedro

Unit III: Family Ties

Families

Who is in your family? When you think of your family, you probably think of your mother, father, sisters or brothers, and you! There can be many other people in a family. Your grandparents, aunts, uncles, and cousins are all relatives. They are all a part of your family, too.

Years ago, most families lived in one place. Many people lived and worked in the same town all their lives. Their sons or daughters lived there, too. Children often built houses near their parents' homes. Younger people learned from older people. Younger generations could care for parents and grandparents as they got older.

Today, families often live far apart. Sons and daughters move away. Often they find opportunities for jobs in other states. Travel is faster and easier. Leaving home is less difficult, and people can fly home quickly. Easier travel has many advantages. But families have grown apart. Old people often live alone. They do not have the support they once had. It is easy for families to lose touch.

Many people write letters to keep in touch. They call on the telephone. Advances in communication help, too. People send computer mail. They send faxes. Staying in touch is important. It makes people feel close even when many miles separate them. Distance is only one of the things that have changed families. People of long ago would be amazed to see the families of today!

Go on to next page.

Directions

Read each clue. Choose a word from the Word List that best fits each clue. Write the words in the puzzle.

Word List

grandparents   relatives   generations   advances
opportunities   support   advantages   communication

ACROSS:

3. people who are related
4. sending and receiving messages
7. help
8. your parents' parents

DOWN:

1. chances
2. progress; forward movement
5. groups of people all born during a certain time
6. things that put one person in a better position than another

Unit III: Family Ties

Too Hot or Not?

"How hot do you think it is today?"
    I heard my mother ask.
I looked at the thermometer;
    that was an easy task.
"It's seventy-two," I called out loud.
    "That's not too hot at all."
"Seventy-two!" she cried in surprise.
    "Oh! That's inside in the hall.
I want you to know how hot it is
    outside in the sun.
I was out there with our neighbors,
    and it's melting everyone!"
I hadn't been outside at all.
    (I just got up, you see.)
She's been out there and knows it's hot.
    So why does she ask me?
It must be very hot indeed
    to make our neighbors melt.
Did they drip like candles made of wax?
    I wonder how that felt.
"Maybe it's ninety in the sun—
    maybe a hundred and ten.
I'm going out to play," I said,
    "and I can tell you then."
I'll get too hot and start to melt,
    I'll play beneath some tree;
but how can knowing a number
    tell me how hot to be?

Go on to next page.

Directions

Answer each question about the poem. Circle the letter in front of the correct answer.

1. When Mother says that the neighbors are melting, she means that they _____.
   a. have all gone inside
   b. are feeling very warm
   c. are burning candles
   d. have disappeared before her eyes

2. It is seventy-two degrees _____.
   a. under the tree
   b. out in the sun
   c. under the covers
   d. inside in the hall

3. Mother was outside with the neighbor _____.
   a. talking about the weather
   b. lighting candles
   c. looking at the thermometer
   d. playing under a tree

4. The boy telling the story has just _____.
   a. been talking to the neighbors
   b. finished melting some candles
   c. gotten out of his bed
   d. come in from playing outside

5. The boy thinks that the best way to know how hot it is outside is to _____.
   a. ask the neighbors
   b. read a thermometer outside
   c. stay inside all day
   d. go out and see how he feels

44

The Museum

One wintry Saturday morning, Ramonda and her mother stepped onto a bus to go downtown. Ramonda had heard many stories about everything there was to see. She had never spent the whole day in the city. She couldn't wait to arrive at the museum, which was where they would spend the day. Her friend Lisa had visited many places in the city. Ramonda never tired of hearing about them.

"Aren't we there yet?" she asked.

"It won't be long now," her mother assured her.

When they finally stepped onto the sidewalk, Ramonda seemed more overwhelmed than excited. The building was gigantic!

"In this building are some of the finest works of art in the world," said her mother. "You will not be able to choose what to look at first."

Ramonda was quite artistic. Her favorite hobbies were drawing and painting. After reading the signs, she begged her mother to start upstairs where the paintings were found.

After a full day of looking at wonderful art exhibits, they had seen only a fraction of what was in the museum. Ramonda's mother purchased special brushes in the gift shop. It was the perfect conclusion to Ramonda's day. She and her mother boarded the bus and returned home. Ramonda had very special memories of her day in the city.

Go on to next page.

Directions

Rewrite each sentence. Use a word with the same meaning from the Word List in place of the underlined words.

Word List
assured   fraction   gigantic   purchased

1. Ramonda was <u>told not to worry</u> by her mother when she said, "It won't be long now."

_____

2. The museum was <u>huge</u>.

_____

3. Ramonda and her mother only saw a <u>part</u> of the museum.

_____

4. Ramonda's mother <u>bought</u> brushes at the gift shop.

_____

Choose the word that best fits each sentence. Write the word in the blank.

5. Ramonda was _____ by the museum.
   overloaded   overwhelmed   frightened

6. She and her mother looked at many beautiful _____.
   exhibits   clothes   exits

7. Ramonda was _____.
   artful   awful   artistic

8. The brushes were the perfect _____ to her day.
   beginning   conclusion   confusing

The Best Present

Anita was born on Leap Year Day, February 29. Since that day only comes once every four years, this was going to be a special birthday party. Grandma and Grandpa were driving up from Tennessee that morning, and Anita sat at the front window waiting to see their car.

By afternoon, the food for the party was ready, and Anita began to help decorate the house. She glanced out the window every time a car went by. Grandma and Grandpa were very late. Mother tried to call them, but she always got a busy signal.

After all the guests had left that night, Anita sat holding the stuffed panda Uncle Bill brought for her. "Maybe Grandma and Grandpa forgot all about my party," she thought. She was very disappointed. It would be four more years before they could come to such a special party again. Then the telephone rang.

"We've had a big snowstorm down here," Grandma said. "All of the telephone lines were down. You must have a lot of snow up north. We'll come and bring your present when it all melts."

"We haven't had any snow at all," Anita said, starting to cry. "This is the best present I've received all day," she said, "knowing that you are all right." Suddenly she realized how worried she had been about Grandma and Grandpa.

Go on to next page.

Directions

Answer each question about the story. Circle the letter in front of the correct answer.

1. Anita is having a special birthday party because _____.
   a. Grandma and Grandpa had never visited before
   b. she was born on Leap Year Day
   c. she is only three years old
   d. people often forget about her birthday

2. Anita keeps looking out the window to see _____.
   a. the snow coming down
   b. what presents people are bringing
   c. if Grandma and Grandpa have arrived
   d. if the sun will shine on her birthday

3. Mother cannot reach Grandma and Grandpa by phone because _____.
   a. the telephone lines are down in Tennessee
   b. they are trying to call Anita
   c. the phone in Anita's house is not working
   d. they are in their car driving north

4. Anita decides that her best present is _____.
   a. the one Grandma and Grandpa will bring
   b. the stuffed panda she gets from Uncle Bill
   c. a heavy snowfall in her town
   d. learning that Grandma and Grandpa are safe

5. Anita starts crying because she _____.
   a. is too old to have a stuffed toy
   b. has been hoping that it would snow in her town
   c. has been so worried about Grandma and Grandpa
   d. is angry at Grandma and Grandpa

City Summer

This is supposed to be an assignment about what I did last summer. I'm not sure I feel like writing about it. I guess I have to tell you why. Last spring, my mom told me I was going to spend the summer with my dad. I was not keen on that arrangement. My dad lives in the city. I like it out here where I can ride my bike to the beach and hang out with my friends. I didn't want to stay in the city all summer and breathe fumes and be bored. Mom would not debate her decision, however, so in June, I hopped on a plane and took the short flight to my dad's.

As it turned out, summer in the city wasn't bad at all. I'm not proud of my behavior when I first arrived. I was angry and disappointed, but Dad understood how I felt and he didn't push me. After a while, I decided it was boring to be mad all the time, so I started acting more like a human being. I'm glad I did. Dad and I went to all kinds of neat places. We went to a lot of ball games, which was fun for both of us. We also checked out the museums. I've never seen so much art in one place! We spent a day at the aquarium and went to all kinds of restaurants where I tried foods that I never knew existed!

About halfway through August, Dad started to get tired fast. He wasn't interested in doing much, so we'd sit around talking. I guess I hadn't known much about Dad's life. Our discussions made me think about him as a kid like me and I realized we had a lot in common. One day, Dad told me to call a cab. He was holding his stomach and breathing heavily, and he looked pale and scared. When the cab arrived, we went to the hospital, where Mom met us a few hours later.

Dad is still in the hospital and may never come out. Mom knew he was sick. That's why she insisted on my staying with him all summer. They didn't tell me about Dad's illness because Dad wanted me to enjoy  myself and not spend my time worrying about him. Well, I did enjoy my summer. It was both the best and the worst summer I'll ever have. I didn't think I'd want to write about it, but now I'm glad I did.

Go on to next page.

Directions

Think about the passage you read. Then fill in the blanks of the following paragraph with words from the Word List.

Word List

keen   fumes   discussions   illness
debate   assignment   arrangement   behavior

The writer is doing a school **1)** _____. He writes that he was

not **2)** _____ to go to the city. He did not care for the

3) _____ his mother had made. He did not want to breathe

4) _____ all summer, but his mother would not

5) _____ her decision. The writer's **6)** _____ was not

good when he first arrived at his dad's. Before he found out about his dad's

7) _____, they had many **8)** _____ that taught the

writer much about his father's life.

A fact is something that has actually happened or that is actually true. An opinion is what someone thinks, which may or may not be true. Write *fact* **or** *opinion* **in front of each sentence about the passage.**

9. _____ The writer wanted to spend the summer near the beach.

10. _____ The city is a boring place to spend the summer.

11. _____ The writer's mother is mean.

12. _____ The writer's parents did not want him to worry.

13. _____ The writer and his father went to many ball games.

Memorial Day

Memorial Day was one of Junie's favorite holidays. She loved the parade and the ceremony in the town square. The band played taps and "The Star Spangled Banner." Now that she was older, she understood the ceremony better. She felt sad and grateful for the soldiers who had died. Afterward, Junie got to see all her relatives as they gathered at her house for a barbecue. She liked the way the holiday seemed to signal the beginning of summer. There were always a few weeks of school after Memorial Day, but they flew right by. Then it was vacation time!

This year, Junie was ten. The town parade did not seem as long or as grand as it had when she was younger, but she still liked it. As always, her grandparents, aunts, uncles, and cousins gathered at her parents' house. Everyone brought all kinds of salads, desserts, and other treats. Junie's Uncle Jess was there. He always brought a present for Junie and her brother, Adam. This was usually the only time of year they got to see him. He liked to make it more special. Last year, he had brought them a rubber raft for the stream. The year before they had gotten a tent for camping in the backyard. She couldn't wait to see what he would bring this year.

Junie, Adam, and their cousins played games of tag and baseball. They told each other stories about what had been going on in their lives since the last gathering. Then it was time to eat. Later, everyone had finished eating and was relaxing and talking. Uncle Jess looked at Junie and Adam. Junie and Adam looked at each other with barely concealed excitement. They followed their uncle to the back of his truck. When everyone saw Junie and Adam again, they were riding a tandem bicycle. It was the best present yet! Everyone took turns riding it up and down the long driveway for the rest of the afternoon. When the day was over, Junie and Adam rode down the drive with each car, waving and calling, "Good-bye!," until each one was out of sight.

Go on to next page.

Directions

Answer each question about the story. Circle the letter in front of the correct answer.

1. What did Junie like about Memorial Day?
   a. She liked to be in the parade.
   b. She liked to see her relatives.
   c. She liked going to her uncle's house.
   d. She liked making the desserts.

2. What is the meaning of *concealed*?
   a. destroyed
   b. excited
   c. hidden
   d. found

3. Why did Uncle Jess bring a present for Junie and Adam?
   a. It was their birthday.
   b. They asked for one.
   c. Everyone brought presents.
   d. He didn't see them often.

4. What is special about a *tandem* bicycle?
   a. Two people can ride it.
   b. It has four wheels.
   c. Three people can ride it.
   d. The pedals move by themselves.

5. Junie and Adam probably live _____.
   a. in the city
   b. in an apartment
   c. in the country
   d. downtown

Enough Gloves

Quinn was shopping in the department store when he saw a woman shaking her finger at the little boy. "He must have done something really bad," Quinn thought, moving down the aisle to hear what she was saying.

"This is the last pair of gloves I'm going to buy you this winter!" the woman said firmly, shaking her finger on one hand and a pair of gloves in the other. "I mean it! If you lose this pair, you can just go around with your hands in your pockets the rest of the winter!"

"Boy, she's really mean," Quinn thought, glaring at the boy's mother.

"What would you do?" the woman almost shouted at Quinn. "This is the third pair of gloves I've had to buy for him this winter! He had each pair a few days and then came home without them! He has to learn to respect things and take good care of them."

"Makes sense to me," Quinn said. And to tell the truth, it did, now that she had explained. "How come you're always losing your gloves?" he asked the boy with a nudge after the mother moved on down the aisle.

"Didn't lose any gloves," the kid said. "Billy and Roscoe had cold hands, and I knew their mothers couldn't afford to get them any."

Go on to next page.

Directions

Answer each question about the story. Circle the letter in front of the correct answer.

1. Quinn moves closer to the woman and her son because Quinn _____.
   a. wants to know what the boy has done wrong
   b. is afraid that the woman will damage the gloves
   c. feels sorry for the woman
   d. knows the little boy

2. Quinn glares at the woman because he thinks she is _____.
   a. going to spank the boy
   b. not the boy's mother
   c. making too big a deal out of gloves
   d. going to say something very important

3. The mother is in the store to _____.
   a. find out what Quinn thinks
   b. find her son's lost gloves
   c. look for Billy's and Roscoe's mothers
   d. buy her son a pair of gloves

4. After the boy's mother explains, Quinn thinks that _____.
   a. she is a very mean woman
   b. the boy needs to learn a lesson
   c. the boy should have all the gloves he wants
   d. the mother should buy mittens instead

5. The boy does not have the first two pairs of gloves because _____.
   a. he lost them playing after school
   b. he felt sorry for his friends
   c. his mother gave them away
   d. he did not like wearing them

Play Ball!

It was a sunny Saturday, and Mark and two of his friends had gone to the neighborhood park to play. Mark was lying in the grass on a hill, lazily tossing a ball into the air and catching it in his glove. Phil and Daniel had run to the playground to spin each other on the tire swing. Shortly, they came back to the hill.

"Hey, Mark," said Phil, panting, "you should see this new kid over there. He thinks he's too good to talk to anybody."

"Yeah," said Daniel. "He definitely has an attitude problem. Come on, let's play some ball."

Mark sat up and looked over at the playground. There was a boy there, sitting on the monkey bars, watching him. Out of curiosity, Mark waved, and the boy waved back. Mark didn't think he seemed very stuck-up at all. Then he had an idea.

"Let's ask that kid to play with us," he said to Phil. "We could use another guy to shag balls."

"Him?" asked Phil doubtfully. "He won't play."

Mark thought he'd try it anyway, so he waved to the boy again. Then he waved his arm, signaling the boy to come to the field. The boy clambered down from the monkey bars and ran over.

"Want to play?" asked Mark.

The boy nodded eagerly, smiling. Mark looked at Phil and Daniel, who shrugged their shoulders. "Well, he wasn't so friendly before," Daniel muttered.

The boy tapped Daniel on the shoulder, and Daniel looked at him questioningly. Then the boy pointed to his ears and shook his head.

"You can't hear?" asked Daniel. The boy nodded. "Sorry," said Daniel. "I apologize. We thought you were being a jerk. Now I feel like a jerk! Here," he said, handing the boy a bat, "you're up first!"

Go on to next page.

Name_____   Date_____

Directions ─────────────────────────

Choose the word that best fits each sentence. Write the word in the blank.

1. Daniel said the boy on the monkey bars had an _____ problem.

   artistic   attitude   awful

2. Out of _____, Mark waved to the boy.

   carelessness   breath   curiosity

3. The boy _____ down from the monkey bars.

   fell   clambered   jumped

4. When Daniel found out the boy could not hear, he said, "I _____."

   apologize   forgot   agree

Write *true* or *false* next to each sentence.

5. _____ The boys were going to play baseball.

6. _____ The new boy could not see.

7. _____ Daniel and Phil thought the boy was unfriendly.

8. _____ Mark wanted the boy to play with them.

9. _____ The boy did not want to play.

10. _____ Daniel felt sorry for what he had said.

Unit IV: You Never Know...
Improving Reading Comprehension 4, SV 5802-7

Sylvia's Bear

Once there was a very rich girl who seemed to have everything she could ever want. She had closets full of clothes, most of which she never wore. She had an entire room just to hold all her toys, many of which she never played with. She had every new gadget that was advertised on television or radio for children. One might think that this girl might be spoiled and unpleasant, but she was very sweet and kind. She always shared whatever she had. She often gave things away, too. Her parents just couldn't resist buying her new things because they loved her and she was their only child.

One day the girl got a package in the mail. It contained a small stuffed bear. The bear was made of scraps of material of every color and pattern, and stitched together by hand. It had mismatched button eyes and a little green velvet vest. The note in its pocket said, "Thank You, to Sylvia from L." Sylvia was certain that this bear must be from Lin, a girl in her class at school. Sylvia had given Lin some clothes and toys for her family. She had never expected anything in return. She knew that Lin did not have money for presents. Lin had made this little bear to repay Sylvia's kindness.

It happened that shortly after Sylvia received the bear, there was a terrible fire at her house. Her family had to run out into the night as fire raged through their lovely home. Suddenly, Sylvia ran back into the house. Her parents screamed for her to stop. Soon, Sylvia ran back out the door, unharmed. Her parents demanded to know what she was thinking. They could replace anything she lost in the fire.

"You could not replace this," said Sylvia, holding out the little patched bear. Her parents shook their heads, mystified. But the truth was, the bear meant more to Sylvia than anything else she had ever owned.

Go on to next page.

Name _____   Date _____

Directions

Answer each question about the story. Circle the letter in front of the correct answer.

1. Sylvia could be described as _____.
   a. kind and generous
   b. mean and spoiled
   c. young and beautiful
   d. sweet and poor

2. Where did Sylvia find the bear?
   a. in her desk at school
   b. on her doorstep
   c. in the mail
   d. at the store

3. Why did Lin give Sylvia the bear?
   a. She did not want it anymore.
   b. It was Sylvia's birthday.
   c. She knew that Sylvia needed one.
   d. She wanted to repay Sylvia's kindness.

4. Sylvia's parents told her to stop because _____.
   a. she could have been hurt in the fire
   b. they wanted to go with her
   c. they had a list of things they wanted
   d. it was late at night

5. Why did Sylvia love the little bear more than anything else she owned?
   a. because it was cute
   b. because it was expensive
   c. because Lin made it just for her
   d. because everyone had one

Mystery House

In Darla's neighborhood, there was a house that sat behind a high iron fence. It was surrounded by trees and bushes. The grass was often long and unkempt, but bright flowers grew in the window boxes. The roof needed patching and the porch sagged, but the windows were unbroken and clean. Darla heard many comments about the woman who lived there. People referred to her as crazy, scary, spooky, and all kinds of other things. She never seemed to leave the house, so Darla had no way of knowing just what the woman might be like.

One day at school, Darla met a new girl named Kim. Kim and Darla found that they had much in common. Darla invited Kim to her house that afternoon.

"My Aunt Nola lives on this street," said Kim as they got off the bus. "Let's go see her!"

As the girls walked down the street, it became apparent to Darla that Kim was headed straight toward the strange house! Darla was speechless as they walked up the overgrown path and knocked on the door. It was opened by a smiling woman in a wheelchair who invited them in and gave Kim a big hug. In the backyard, Aunt Nola wheeled down a ramp to the center of a charming garden where she had a table and some chairs. She offered the girls lemonade and cookies. An hour flew right by, and Darla hoped as they left that Kim would bring her back again soon.

Go on to next page.

Name _____   Date _____

Directions

Rewrite each sentence. Use a word with the same meaning from the Word List in place of the underlined words.

Word List

unkempt   speechless   unbroken   apparent

1. The windows in the house were <u>whole</u>.

_____

2. The lawn was <u>a mess</u>.

_____

3. It became <u>clear</u> that Kim was heading straight to the strange house.

_____

4. Darla was <u>unable to speak</u> as they walked down the path.

_____

Choose the word that best fits each sentence. Write the word in the blank.

5. People _____ to the woman as crazy and scary.
  realized   referred   talked

6. Darla heard their _____.
  contents   thoughts   comments

7. The path was _____ with weeds.
  overgrown   overdone   cleared

8. The woman took them to her _____ garden.
  caring   vegetable   charming

Unit IV: You Never Know...

Improving Reading Comprehension 4, SV 5802-7

Spilled Milk

A milkmaid was on her way to market, carrying a pail of milk on the top of her head. As she walked along the road in the early morning, she began to turn over in her mind what she would do with the money she would receive for the milk.

"I shall buy some hens from a neighbor," she said to herself, "and they will lay eggs every day, which I shall sell to the pastor's wife. And with the egg money I'll buy myself a new frock and ribbon. Green they should be, for green goes with my complexion best. And in this lovely green gown I will go to the fair. All the young men will strive to have me for a partner. I shall pretend that I don't see them. When they become too insistent I shall disdainfully toss my head—like this."

As the milkmaid spoke she tossed her head back, and down came the pail of milk, spilling all over the ground. And so all her imaginary happiness vanished, and nothing was left but an empty pail and the promise of a scolding when she returned home.

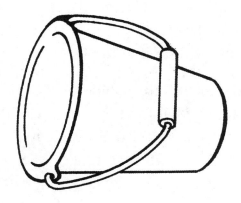

Go on to next page.

Directions ———————————————————————

Answer each questions about the fable. Circle the letter in front of the correct answer.

1. What is the maid taking to sell?
   a. eggs
   b. hens
   c. milk
   d. ribbons

2. What does the maid plan to buy with the money she hopes to get for the eggs?
   a. pretty things to wear
   b. some milk to take home
   c. a new pail to carry milk
   d. something to give to a boy

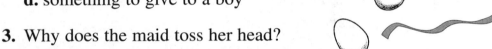

3. Why does the maid toss her head?
   a. to turn and look at a young man
   b. to show that she does not care that she had dropped the pail
   c. to look at a frock and ribbon
   d. to practice how she will do it at the fair

4. Why does the maid expect to be scolded?
   a. because she has stopped at the fair
   b. because she has nothing to show for her trip
   c. for buying herself things with the money she gets
   d. for buying hens that would lay eggs

5. Which of these is the moral of this story?
   a. A disdainful look will catch boys' eyes.
   b. Don't cry over spilled milk.
   c. Don't count your chickens before they hatch.
   d. Never dare to smile at the fair or wear green ribbons in your hair.

Chili Surprise!

One fall afternoon on Manny's family's farm, one of the cows got loose from the pasture and wandered down to the stream. Her foot had become entangled among some branches and she was stuck there in the chilly water. Manny's mother, father, and his older sister Rosa had all gone to the stream to see if they could rescue the cow. Manny's mother told him to stay in the house in case anyone called. One of their neighbors did come by, and Manny sent him down to the stream. He hated missing all the excitement, and he sat with his chin in his hands for a while feeling disappointed and angry.

As time went on, Manny began to get hungry. It occurred to him that his mother had not yet started dinner. He thought of an idea to surprise everyone. They all treated Manny as if he couldn't do anything just because he was the youngest in the family, but he knew there was something he could do. He would just have to be careful!

Manny's parents, with their neighbor's help, were able to free the cow. She had only some scrapes on her leg. They came back to the house cold, dirty, and hungry. A heavenly aroma was wafting from the kitchen.

"That smells like chili!" exclaimed Manny's mother. "Manny, did someone bring us chili?"

Manny came around the corner and smiled at his mother. "No one brought us chili, Mom," he said. "I made it!"

Everyone was shocked and surprised that Manny could have made dinner all by himself. They tasted the chili and pronounced it delicious. Manny's mother asked him how he could have known what to do.

"It was simple," said Manny. "I've watched you make chili a hundred times. I knew you wouldn't let me do it if I asked, but I wanted to do something to help, and I knew I could make dinner if I tried!"

Manny's family and their neighbor all sat down and had their delightful surprise chili dinner, and from then on, no one knew what they might expect from Manny. He was probably full of surprises!

Go on to next page.

Directions

**Read each clue. Choose a word from the Word List that fits each clue.
Write the words in the puzzle.**

Word List

pasture   occurred   heavenly   aroma
wafting   pronounced   entangled   delightful

ACROSS:
1. floating
3. declared
6. wonderful
7. caught

DOWN:
2. scent
3. field for grazing
4. came to mind
5. very pleasing

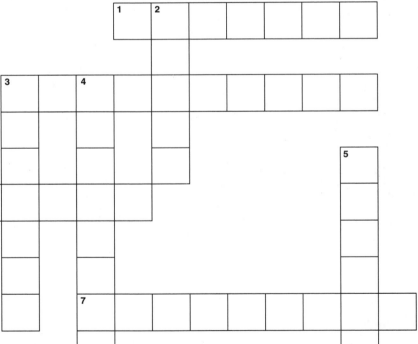

Hats Off!

The hat had been given to Mrs. Beanwater many years before. It was the kind of pink that shows up a long way on a sunny day. It had a wide brim with little red cherries made of clay and a garden of tiny white flowers stuck in the band all around the brim.

The brim was a faded pink, even though the hat had always sat on a dark shelf. As soon as the friend who gave it to her left, Mrs. Beanwater sighed and said, "What a dreadful hat! What a frightfully ugly hat!"

The hat would still be on the shelf if it weren't for the crows. Mrs. Beanwater needed a hat for the scarecrow she made this summer. The friend who gave it to her had moved away, and Mrs. Beanwater was certain the hat would frighten anything that saw it.

As it turned out, the crows loved it; and so did Miss Dallywinkle. The crows sat along the brim picking at the clay cherries, and Miss Dallywinkle came to Mrs. Beanwater's door.

"Since your scarecrow's lovely hat isn't working," Miss Dallywinkle said, "I wonder if you might swap it for a hat of mine that I'm certain will scare the crows."

No one ever found out. Starting the very next day the townspeople began admiring a black felt hat that Mrs. Beanwater wore from that day on; and the poor scarecrow, who wore it for less than an hour, has gone hatless ever since.

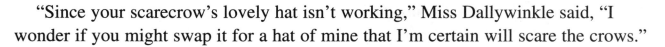

Go on to next page.

© Steck-Vaughn Company

Unit IV: You Never Know...

Improving Reading Comprehension 4, SV 5802-7

Directions

Answer each question about the story. Circle the letter in front of the correct answer.

1. When it comes to hats, Mrs. Beanwater and Miss Dallywinkle seem to have _____.
   a. too many for their own good
   b. a difference of opinion
   c. a liking for the same colors
   d. many hats with flowers on them

2. We do not know if the black felt hat would frighten the crows because _____.
   a. Mrs. Beanwater decides to wear it
   b. Miss Dallywinkle decides to keep it
   c. the scarecrow refuses to wear it
   d. someone in town steals it

3. Miss Dallywinkle offers to swap hats because she _____.
   a. thinks the scarecrow looks silly in it
   b. has given the pink hat to Mrs. Beanwater
   c. really likes the pink hat
   d. feels sorry for Mrs. Beanwater

4. The black felt hat is admired by _____.
   a. both Miss Dallywinkle and Mrs. Beanwater
   b. neither Miss Dallywinkle nor Mrs. Beanwater
   c. only Miss Dallywinkle
   d. Mrs. Beanwater

5. The crows in this story seem to agree with _____.
   a. Miss Dallywinkle
   b. Mrs. Beanwater
   c. neither Miss Dallywinkle nor Mrs. Beanwater
   d. the townspeople

Good Guy

Bobby guessed that they were going on a Sunday drive, so when they pulled into Top Breed Kennels, he was surprised. "We promised you a dog," his mother said, "and today you can pick one."

The kennel sold poodle and collie puppies, and as Bobby walked down the aisle between the pens with the beautiful pups, he wanted them all. The dogs yipped and came to the screen to lick his fingers. Bobby said that picking one dog would be like freeing it, but the man who sold the dogs said, "All of these pups will find homes. Today, people want pure-blooded dogs. These dogs will all have new homes within weeks."

Bobby's father suggested that they look at other dogs before Bobby made his choice, so they visited other kennels. Bobby saw Airedales, cocker spaniels, and so many other kinds of dogs that he felt confused. The last stop had a sign reading "County Humane Society."

Inside, a full grown dog with long ears and uneven dark spots stood, slowly wagging its stubby tail and watching with big, brown eyes as Bobby looked in the pens. "I hope someone picks him soon," the lady on duty said. "He's such a nice dog. He's a mongrel, but such a good guy; and we can't keep him much longer."

Outside, the dog wiggled with glee as Bobby led him on a leash to the car. "Come on, Good Guy," Bobby said, "we're going to show you your new home."

Go on to next page.

Directions

Answer each question about the story. Circle the letter in front of the correct answer.

1. The dogs at Top Breed Kennels will all find homes because _____.
   a. they are all pure-blooded
   b. Bobby will choose them all
   c. they are all Airedales
   d. the man is a good salesman

2. Bobby thinks the puppies must feel like _____.
   a. no one likes them
   b. people will hurt them
   c. they are in prison
   d. Bobby is being unkind

3. Bobby feels confused because he _____.
   a. does not want any of the dogs he sees
   b. cannot read the signs on the kennels
   c. is not sure that he can have a dog
   d. sees so many kinds of dogs

4. Bobby picks Good Guy because he is a nice dog that _____.
   a. everyone wants
   b. might not find a home
   c. is bigger than the puppies
   d. is pure-blooded

5. Bobby gets the idea for his dog's name from _____.
   a. a sign that they pass
   b. something his father says
   c. the lady at the Humane Society
   d. the man at Top Breed Kennels

Animals in Space

Animals have done many surprising things. Some have been heroes. Some have been stars in movies and on television shows. Animals help people in many ways. Animals have even helped people to study space travel.

Since 1957, many animals have gone into space. They have helped scientists answer questions about space travel. They have helped make space travel safe for humans. The first animal in space was a dog named Laika. She was the first Earth creature to orbit Earth. She showed that humans could survive space travel. Unfortunately, Laika did not survive her journey. She died when her capsule ran out of oxygen.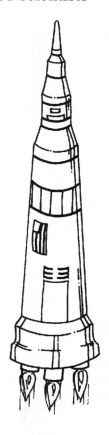

Since then, other animals have followed Laika's path. Almost all have been safely recovered. Scientists have sent four more dogs and several chimpanzees and monkeys into space. Of these, only Gordo, a squirrel monkey, was lost. His capsule failed to float upon landing in the ocean.

All of these animals have risked their lives to help humans travel safely. We have no way of knowing what they may have thought about their journeys. Maybe Enos, a chimp that orbited the earth twice in 1961, "spoke" for all of them. It is said that when he was taken from his capsule, he jumped up and down with joy. Then he shook the hands of the people who had rescued him. It seems clear that he was glad to be back on Earth!

Go on to next page.

Directions

Think about the passage you read. Then fill in the blanks of the following paragraph with words from the Word List. (Remember to use a capital letter to begin a sentence.)

Word List

survive   chimp   oxygen   unfortunately
risked   orbited   capsule   recovered

Many animals have **1)** _____ their lives to help people study

space. A dog named Laika **2)** _____ Earth in 1957.

3) _____, Laika did not **4)** _____. She died when

her **5)** _____ ran out of **6)** _____. Enos, a

7) _____, orbited Earth twice in 1961. Enos was

8) _____ safely.

Use the Word List above to choose the correct word for each meaning. Write your choice on the line.

9. got back _____

10. went around _____

11. to live _____

12. an invisible gas_____

13. without luck _____

14. put in danger _____

15. part of a spacecraft_____

16. a kind of ape_____

Scaredy Cat

In the darkness Pepper couldn't see his friends sitting around him in Betty's backyard as he made up his story. Meg had just finished one about Charlotte, an English girl who was lost and came to a big, dingy castle. Charlotte went from room to room following strange noises made by squeaking shutters or broken curtain rods scraping against windows.

Pepper decided to continue Meg's story. "Charlotte heard moans from below," he said. "She started down some dark stone stairs leading to an old, smelly cellar. She put her hand on the wall to feel her way, and it was wet and cold and sticky."

The story must have scared Betty's black cat, Andy. He got up to go to the front yard and brushed against Meg's leg. "Agghhh! Get out of here!" Meg cried.

"At the bottom of the stairs," Pepper continued, "Charlotte turned a corner toward a flickering light. Her blood turned ice cold when she saw..."

"Yeeee-ike! Help! Help!" someone screamed from the front of the house. The children ran out front, almost expecting to find poor Charlotte. There stood Mrs. Winters, a neighbor, pointing to a big shopping bag she had dropped on the sidewalk. "Some creature jumped into my bag," she shrieked. Two yellow eyes slowly peeped up from inside the bag.

"It's only Andy," Betty said.

Go on to next page.

Directions

Answer each question about the story. Circle the letter in front of the correct answer.

1. Pepper and his friends are _____.
   a. lost somewhere in England
   b. making up spooky stories
   c. trapped in a smelly cellar
   d. looking for Betty's cat

2. The person who is in the castle is _____.
   a. Betty
   b. Andy
   c. Meg
   d. Charlotte

3. Meg is frightened when she _____.
   a. feels the cat brush her leg
   b. hears creaking shutters
   c. comes to the bottom of the stairs
   d. sees that Andy is in the bag

4. When Mrs. Winters screams, the children probably feel _____.
   a. angry that Andy has interrupted the story
   b. bored with the story about Charlotte
   c. sorry that the story is over
   d. frightened for poor Charlotte

5. The children get together to tell stories because they _____.
   a. like to play with Betty's cat
   b. are afraid to be alone in the dark
   c. enjoy hearing scary stories
   d. want to trick Mrs. Winters

Bedelia

Al could not remember life before Bedelia arrived. It seemed that the big, gentle dog had always been with him. Al could remember all the way back to his fourth birthday. He could see Bedelia then, sitting on the floor next to his chair as he opened his presents. He could remember his first day of kindergarten, when Bedelia stayed in the car and he went into school. He could remember the first summer in their new house, when Bedelia got a new house of her own out in the yard.

In Al's memories, Bedelia was always full grown. He never thought of her as small, although he knew she was once a puppy. She was always tall and slim, with flowing red hair. Even now that Al was growing, Bedelia was still a big dog. She was as high as his chest, and she could raise her head to look right at him with her wide, brown eyes.

Go on to next page.

Directions

Answer each question about the story. Circle the letter in front of the correct answer.

1. Bedelia is a _____.
   a. person
   b. dog
   c. cat
   d. fox

2. Al is probably _____.
   a. a young child
   b. an adult
   c. ten or eleven years old
   d. an old man

3. Which of these best describes Al's feelings for Bedelia?
   a. dislike
   b. fear
   c. wonder
   d. love

Write *true* or *false* next to each sentence.

5. _____ Bedelia was always full grown.

6. _____ Al took Bedelia into kindergarten with him.

7. _____ Bedelia had a house of her own.

8. _____ Bedelia had flowing red hair.

9. _____ Al wishes for a different dog.

Not a Word Bird

When I was very young, my family had a parakeet that lived in a cage in the dining room. We had never had a bird for a pet before, and I wasn't sure it was going to be much fun. My older brothers had begged my mother to get "Ricky," though. They kept telling me how much fun he would be and that we could even teach him to talk. "Now, when did you ever hear a cat or a dog talk?" they asked in their most demanding older-brother way.

"Yeah, but I can't take a bird for a walk. I can't sit by the fire and cuddle it on my lap."

"Oh, you'll see. It will be a lot of fun to have Ricky. We can let him out of the cage. He'll fly around, and we'll play with him. He'll sit on your shoulder, and you can smooth his little feathers. You'll like him a lot ... just like a cat or dog."

So we got the parakeet. Ricky was not a friendly bird as my brothers had promised. I tried talking to him, repeating and repeating. Then I'd put my finger up to the cage, trying to make contact, and every time he would nip at my finger. I kept telling myself that he had to get to know me or he was just afraid. Ricky never learned to talk, either. I remember thinking that when he learned to talk, I would tell him not to bite me. When I was old enough to realize the mistake I had made, I had to laugh to myself. But it wasn't so fantastic, really. As children, we think that talking and understanding are very closely connected.

Go on to next page.

Directions

Answer each question about the story. Circle the letter in front of the correct answer.

1. What kind of pet did the author want?
   a. a parakeet
   b. a canary
   c. a dog or cat
   d. a mouse

2. Who wanted to get a parakeet?
   a. the author's mother
   b. the author's sisters
   c. the author's brothers
   d. the author

3. How was "Ricky" not what the family expected?
   a. He could not fly.
   b. He did not talk.
   c. He was not a bird.
   d. He was friendly.

4. Why did the author laugh to himself when he thought about telling "Ricky" not to bite anymore?
   a. The author knew he was foolish.
   b. The author knew the bird would not listen.
   c. The author realized that the bird would not understand.
   d. The author realized that the bird could not hear.

5. What kind of pet did the author probably get when he was older?
   a. a dog
   b. a parakeet
   c. a gerbil
   d. some fish

A Cat for Company

Ever since she could remember, Elizabeth had wanted to have a cat. She had stuffed cats, porcelain cats with their kittens, pictures of cats, and books about cats, but she did not have a cat of her own. She asked for one at every opportunity, but there always seemed to be some reason why she could not yet have a cat.

Finally, when Elizabeth turned ten, her parents gave her a certificate good for one cat. Elizabeth was thrilled. The next day she went with her father to the local pet shelter to pick out a kitten. It wasn't easy. They were all so cute! Elizabeth wished she could take them all home. At last she chose a pretty kitten. It was brown with flecks of gold, a gold stripe on its nose, and one gold foot. She brought it home and named it Specks. From the beginning, Specks knew that Elizabeth was her person. She always slept on Elizabeth's bed and jumped up on her lap when she sat down.

Shortly after getting Specks, Elizabeth's family moved to another state. Specks made the journey on Elizabeth's lap, curled up on a pillow and perfectly content. Elizabeth was glad to have Specks at her new home. She had to make new friends and go to a new school. It was nice to have the same old friend at home to be her companion when she felt lonely.

Whenever Elizabeth did make a new friend, she couldn't wait to show off Specks. Her friends all thought Specks was beautiful. She had grown into a petite but pretty adult cat. In addition to her gold toe and the stripe on her nose, now she had a gold patch on her chest, too. Elizabeth could hardly remember what life had been like before Specks!

Go on to next page.

Directions

Read each clue. Choose a word from the Word List that fits each clue. Write the words in the puzzle.

Word List

certificate   companion   addition   flecks
petite   content   local   porcelain

ACROSS:

2. nearby
4. small bits
6. adding to
8. an official paper

DOWN:

1. a hard white material
3. one who stays with another
5. happy
7. small

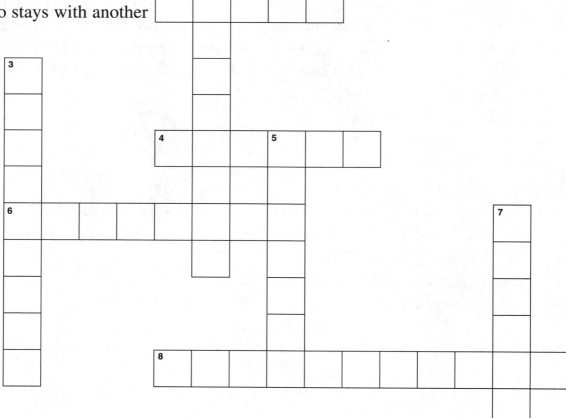

Unit V: All About Animals
Improving Reading Comprehension 4, SV 5802-7

Animal Show

The moon shone like a huge, silver spotlight over the woods. The edges of the bare limbs were painted white against the night hanging behind the woods like a huge, soft curtain.

"Who, whoooo, whoo," a voice called like an announcer or narrator sitting somewhere out there.

"I know who," Sylvia said. She was sitting on the deck behind her grandfather's house, looking out at the woods. "You're the old, wise owl, that's who. What I'm waiting to see are the other actors."

Soon she saw some. Little white flashes came waving out of the woods like tiny flags. The deer were coming up to feed in the tall grass.

"Oh," Sylvia thought, "I hope I get a glimpse of the sly, old fox again tonight. Or maybe the raccoon family will slip up like robbers to raid the trash cans." She sat very still and enjoyed the gentle night breeze. It felt like Grandma was there again fanning Sylvia with the old wicker fan.

The deer made a sudden thumping clatter as they ran for the woods. Along the edge of the woods, Sylvia could barely make out the shape of the wily fox, zigzagging along with its nose vacuuming up scents from the ground.

Go on to next page.

Directions

Answer each question about the story. Circle the letter in front of the correct answer.

1. The moon reminds Sylvia of a _____.
   a. bucket of white paint
   b. hole in the curtain
   c. big spotlight
   d. wise old owl

2. Sylvia thinks of the woods as a _____.
   a. jungle
   b. stage
   c. picture
   d. TV screen

3. The tails of the deer are compared to _____.
   a. fans
   b. lightning
   c. flags
   d. actors

4. The deer run into the woods because _____.
   a. the fox comes out
   b. Sylvia makes a noise
   c. the owl frightens them
   d. they have finished their act

5. The fox's nose is compared to a _____.
   a. waving flag
   b. robber's flashlight
   c. perfume bottle
   d. vacuum cleaner

Stranded

I don't know what ever made me think I could do this on my own. If I get out of this, I really will have to sit down and have a talk with myself about how I get into foolish situations. I always think that I have to show someone that I can do it. I don't stop and think. I just plunge ahead when someone says, "I don't think you can do that yet." Hearing that is like seeing a starting flag go down at the start of a race. I'm off! If I keep doing this my whole life, I don't think I'll live to be thirteen!

I'm really feeling tired, but I can't drift off to sleep. Anything could happen. I just can't seem to keep my eyes open. Maybe if I just close my eyes for a few minutes while I'm drifting.

Wait a minute! Where am I? Oh, I remember. "Expert sailor lost at sea."

"He knew so much about sailing. How could he have gotten into such trouble? He's never been seen or heard of since."

Wait. Do I see something way over there or have I drifted off in my mind, too? I've read about stranded sailors losing their minds. No, wait. That is something. I think it's a boat. It seems to be getting larger, I think. I've got to keep my eye on it. Can't lose sight of it. Yes, it is a boat. I think it might be coming this way. I can almost see who's on it now. I think it's my sailing instructor and my mom! Gosh, do they think I need rescuing? Don't they know that sailors often have to drift and wait for the wind to come up? Oh well, it will probably make them feel better to know I'm really okay.

Go on to next page.

© Steck-Vaughn Company

Unit VI: Mystery and Adventure
Improving Reading Comprehension 4, SV 5802-7

Directions _____

Answer each question about the story. Circle the letter in front of the correct answer.

1. The author is probably _____.
   a. thirteen years old
   b. an adult
   c. five years old
   d. almost thirteen

2. The writer thinks he gets into trouble because _____.
   a. he does not stop and think
   b. he likes to race
   c. he is tired
   d. he is stranded

3. Where is the writer?
   a. in a canoe on a river
   b. in a hot-air balloon
   c. in a sailboat on the ocean
   d. at a racetrack

4. What does *stranded* mean?
   a. broken off
   b. sent away
   c. sinking in water
   d. being in a helpless position

5. How do the writer's feelings change at the end of the passage?
   a. He is still afraid and angry with himself.
   b. He acts as if he does not need help because he knows he is safe.
   c. He becomes worried about his mother and instructor.
   d. He feels proud that he has survived.

Ghostly Towns

They are mysterious, strange, often spooky, and sometimes beautiful. Ghost towns are the remains of once bustling, lively villages. There are hundreds of ghost towns around the United States. Some are on islands. All that is left of most of them are cellar holes, graveyards, and a few decaying buildings. The roads may be overgrown. The wells may be covered over. Without someone to point out certain sites, a person might pass right by them. What happened to these towns? Where did all the people go? Why were these towns started and then left?

Ghost towns exist for several reasons. One of the most common is changes in economics. Many ghost towns started out as busy mill towns or quarry towns. People came to the town to work in the mill or quarry. Then people came who set up bakeries, schools, and shops. Soon, there was a community. But perhaps the resource was used up. Or someone found a better stone to use. Then people stopped buying the product that kept the town going. Soon people began to move away to look for other work. When there were not enough people to support the small businesses, they too closed. Eventually, the town became deserted. Many of the towns that began in the west when people searched for gold were left when there was no gold to be found, or the mines were emptied.

Some reasons for ghost towns are less common. One town in Massachusetts started on a rocky area, inland from the ocean. It was put there partly as protection from pirates. Later, pirates were no longer a threat. People slowly abandoned the town. The town of Flagstaff, Maine, was not only deserted, but also buried under water. This town was flooded to make a reserve water supply for the electric company. The people were forced to move and their houses to be lost for the good of many more people.

When you visit a ghost town, it is interesting to try to imagine what life must have been like for the people who lived there. Often you can find out much from people who still live nearby. There are usually many local tales about ghost towns and some that only add to the mystery.

Go on to next page.

Directions

Think about the passage you read. Then fill in the blanks of the following paragraph with words from the Word List.

Word List

decaying   abandoned   economics   quarry
resource   protection   sites   reserve

Ghost towns are towns that have been **1)** _____. Many towns became

ghost towns because of changes in **2)** _____. If many people in the town

worked at a **3)** _____ and the **4)** _____ that was being mined ran

out, people would have to look somewhere else for work. One town was built away

from the ocean for **5)** _____ from pirates. When pirates were no longer a

problem, the people moved to better places. Another town was flooded to create a

water **6)** _____ for the electric company. All that is left at many

7) _____ are old and **8)** _____ buildings and graveyards.

A fact is something that has actually happened or that is actually true. An opinion is what someone thinks, which may or may not be true. Write *fact* or *opinion* in front of each sentence about the passage.

9. _____ They are mysterious, strange, often spooky, and sometimes
   beautiful.

10. _____ Ghost towns are the remains of once bustling, lively villages.

11. _____ Many ghost towns started out as busy mill towns or quarry
    towns.

12. _____ It was put there partly as protection from pirates.

13. _____ It is interesting to try to imagine what life must have been like.

Castles

Castles can be grand and mysterious places. The high walls, the passages and walkways, and the murky dungeons make castles seem from another world. Castles were not mysterious to those who built and lived in them hundreds of years ago. They were home.

Castles were like small towns. The lord and lady had their family and servants. There were workers and soldiers. There were people who kept up the buildings. There were gardens for growing food. There was usually a village outside the castle walls. The village sometimes helped protect the castle. It may have had a wall around it, too. The village and farmlands supplied the castle with more food.

Castles were built for safety and defense from attack. There were several ways to attack a castle. For each type of attack, the castle soldiers had a plan to fight back. Walls were buried deep in the ground to prevent the digging of tunnels. Moats surrounded many castles as well. There were many small windows, cuts in the stone, and turrets. The soldiers could watch for and shoot arrows at their enemies from these places. They dropped rocks, boiling water, and hot sand onto their attackers. If the enemy put up ladders, they could be pushed away. A castle might be surrounded. This was so that no food could be brought in. The enemy hoped those inside would starve or surrender. Those in the castle made every attempt to keep large supplies of food on hand always.

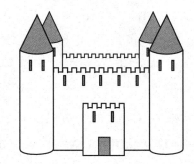

Over the years, castles became less important. Times became more peaceful. Eventually, many castles were abandoned. Their stones were used for building in the surrounding villages. Many other stone castles still stand today. Some have been used as royal palaces.

Go on to next page.

Name _____   Date _____

Directions

Answer each question about the story. Circle the letter in front of the correct answer.

1. Why were castles built?
   a. as a place for lords and ladies to live
   b. so that soldiers could practice fighting
   c. for safety and defense from attack
   d. to keep builders busy

2. Why would the enemy surround a castle?
   a. so that the people inside would starve or surrender
   b. so that no one could attack the castle
   c. so that the soldiers would see all the attackers
   d. so that they could see all the sides

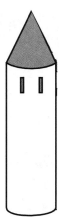

3. Where did the people in a castle get their food?
   a. from visiting ships
   b. they made it all
   c. they grew some and got some from the village
   d. they bought it in cities

4. What might happen to a castle without soldiers?
   a. It would be kept safe by the villagers.
   b. The lord and lady could protect it.
   c. The enemy would be afraid to attack.
   d. The castle would fall quickly to the enemy.

5. How are some castles used today?
   a. They are still used for protection.
   b. They are mostly theme parks.
   c. Some are used as royal palaces.
   d. All of the castles have been destroyed.

Unit VI: Mystery and Adventure
Improving Reading Comprehension 4, SV 5802-7

See Monsters?

Long ago sailors had much to fear from their voyages on the ocean. They did not know the earth was round, so they feared falling off its edge. They heard stories of boiling waters. They heard of huge and menacing sea creatures. Many claimed to have seen them. Reports of sea monsters have not been completely explained away. People continue to see strange sea creatures.

Underwater monsters have been sighted all over the world. They have been seen by all kinds of people. Many people report very similar-looking creatures. They seem to fall into a few categories. Some are snake-like, but they do not move like snakes. Others have large bodies. Some have fins. Others have fish-like tails.

Many people do not believe these stories. They explain the sightings another way. They think people have seen giant squid or an octopus. They say that even seaweed beds or a school of dolphins can cause confusion. Other people cannot dismiss the stories altogether. They note that many of those who claim to see the monsters are intelligent, honest people. Many are seamen who know the water well. They know its natural inhabitants. Believers point out that these monsters could be related to prehistoric sea animals. In later years, people claim to have taken photographs. Could these prove that sea monsters exist?

Do you believe there are huge, strange creatures swimming in our oceans and lakes? As with many strange events, we may have to see it to believe it. That may be an experience some people would choose not to have!

Go on to next page.

Name _____   Date _____

Directions

Read each sentence. Choose a word from the Word List that has the same meaning as the word or words in bold print. Write the word on the line.

Word List

menacing   categories   dismiss   seamen
inhabitants   prehistoric   voyages   squid

1. **Men of the sea** and others have reported sightings of sea creatures for many years. _____

2. Their **trips on the water** were full of the unknown. _____

3. The sea creatures were said to be **dangerous**. _____

4. Sailors know the **creatures that live there** in the sea. _____

5. The creatures people see seem to fall into a few **groups**. _____

6. Some say that people are being confused by giant **sea animals**. _____

7. Others cannot **let go** of the stories that easily. _____

8. They believe the creatures may be relatives of **before the time of recorded history** animals. _____

Write *true* or *false* next to each sentence.

9. _____ Sailors once thought the earth was flat.

10. _____ They captured many sea monsters.

11. _____ People still report sightings of sea monsters.

12. _____ There is proof that sea monsters exist.

13. _____ People claim to have taken pictures of sea monsters.

A New View

An experience does not have to be very big or exciting to be an adventure. You don't have to make a grand discovery or travel far. You can have an adventure every day. Learning something new is an adventure. Exploring a new place in your town or neighborhood can be an adventure.

Every time you learn something new, it makes you grow. It gives you a new piece of knowledge that you can share with other people. How do you learn new things? When you are at school, there are new things to learn every day. Your teacher presents them to you in books, as class work, as research at the library, or as homework. When you are not in school, you continue to learn new things. You ask questions, you watch the news, you read books, and you go places. Sometimes you may go to a new place. Other times you may go to a place you've been to often. Each time, you can learn something new and make the trip an adventure.

Curiosity is what brings us adventure. If we don't wonder about anything, we will not experience much. If you wonder what is on the other side of the hill, you can go and find out. You may wonder what it would be like to try a new food, speak a different language, or live in another time. You can try the food, learn the language, or read a book. Museums are great fun to visit. They can teach us much about how other people have lived.

Every day of our lives is a day to learn and grow. There will always be something more to learn and do. There will always be an adventure waiting around the corner.

Go on to next page.

Directions

Read each question about the story. Circle the letter in front of the correct answer.

1. What is the main idea of this story?
   a. School is an adventure.
   b. Exploring is fun.
   c. Learning is an adventure.
   d. Reading is fun.

2. What is *curiosity*?
   a. wonder
   b. foolishness
   c. adventure
   d. learning

3. What does the story say that a person needs to have an adventure?
   a. a lot of money
   b. to travel far
   c. many friends
   d. curiosity

4. Which of these is *not* mentioned in the story?
   a. trying a new food
   b. learning to fly
   c. speaking a new language
   d. living in another time

5. Which of these is an opinion from the story?
   a. When you are at school, there are new things to learn every day.
   b. If you wonder what is on the other side of the hill, you can go and find out.
   c. Other times you may go to a place you've been to often.
   d. Museums are great fun to visit.

Movie Mystery

Jill and Paul went to the store to rent a movie. Jill was going to get some popcorn and Paul was going to choose the movie. "Remember, Paul," said Jill. "I don't like mysteries!"

When Paul and Jill met in front of the store, she said, "What did you get? Is it a good one? Were there many movies available?"

"Don't worry," said Paul. "It's not a mystery!"

They got to Paul's house, and Paul put the movie into the VCR. There were many previews, and then finally the feature movie started.

"Oh!" said Jill. "Is this a good one? Have you seen this one yet?" As the characters in the movie came on, Jill said, "Who's that? I wonder what she will do" or "I'll bet that man is the one who causes all the trouble!" Then, as the plot moved along, she would say, "Now why did they do that?" or "Don't they know there's a trap there? Why don't they go the other way around?"

Jill asked questions about every detail of the movie. Paul said, "Just watch!" The movie reached its climax; it was the big event that the plot of the movie had been working toward all along. Paul thought all of Jill's questions must have been answered. However, as the credits began to roll, Jill said, "Why didn't they just leave in the first place?"

Paul started to rewind the movie. He said, "Jill, I have never heard so many questions in my life! I think you might as well watch mysteries—for you, every movie is a mystery!"

Go on to next page.

Name_____   Date_____

Directions

Read each clue. Choose a word from the Word List that fits each clue.
Write the words in the puzzle.

Word List
available   previews   feature   plot
rewind   detail   climax   credits

ACROSS:

4. to wind again
6. possible to get
7. a list that tells who did the work in a book or movie
8. the actions and events of a story

DOWN:

1. views of something to come
2. the point of highest interest in a book or movie
3. in film, the main attraction
5. a bit of information

© Steck-Vaughn Company

Unit VI: Mystery and Adventure
Improving Reading Comprehension 4, SV 5802-7

The Trunk

Amy and Andy crept up the attic stairs of their grandfather's house. He didn't mind if they looked around, but each time the children climbed the stairs, they felt a little frightened of the attic. Light came in at each end of the room through the windows, but the old crates, boxes, and furniture there gave the room a spooky feeling. Amy and Andy knew that most of the boxes had been there for many years. Still, something about the attic drew them there.

This time, Amy's eyes were drawn immediately to a trunk in the middle of a clearing on the floor. She did not remember seeing such a trunk on previous visits. Amy went to the trunk and opened the heavy lid. Inside were many odd items. Amy wasn't sure what they were. She reached toward the bottom of the trunk and pulled out a cloak. It looked like something a magician would wear. She put it over her shoulders.

"Hey, Andy!" she called. "Look at me!"

"Where are you?" said Andy. "Amy, stop playing games. Where did you go?"

"Right here, silly!" said Amy. "I'm trying out this cloak!" As she took it off, she reappeared.

The children took turns trying on the cloak, and decided it must be magic. They put it back into the trunk and ran down the stairs to tell their grandfather. When he heard their story, their grandfather laughed. The children insisted that he come up and look at the trunk with them, but when they got back to the attic, the whole trunk was gone! They looked all over the attic for the trunk, but they never found it again. No one but Amy and Adam seemed to believe their story of the cloak. But they couldn't help noticing a twinkle in their grandfather's eye whenever they told the story.

Go on to next page.

Name _____   Date _____

Directions

Answer each question about the story. Circle the letter in front of the correct answer.

1. The children found the trunk in _____.
   a. their grandfather's cellar
   b. their grandfather's garage
   c. their parents' attic
   d. their grandfather's attic

2. The trunk was _____.
   a. something they had seen before
   b. something they had not seen
   c. buried by many old boxes
   d. empty except for the cloak

3. The cloak made Amy _____.
   a. hungry
   b. shrink
   c. disappear
   d. hot

4. When they looked for the trunk again, _____.
   a. it was gone
   b. it was locked shut
   c. it had been moved
   d. it was empty

5. The twinkle in their grandfather's eye probably made the children think that _____.
   a. their grandfather was crying
   b. their grandfather was old
   c. their grandfather had a secret
   d. their grandfather did not believe them

Improving Reading Comprehension
Grade 4

Answer Key

P. 7
1. freeing
2. blooded
3. suggested
4. confused
5. Humane

P. 8
1. Consider
2. imagine
3. protect
4. avenues
5. rutted

P. 9
1. b
2. a
3. c

P. 10
ACROSS
3. eventually
4. economics
5. quarry
DOWN
1. resource
2. product

P. 12
1. b
2. c
3. a
4. d
5. a

P. 14
1. American
2. research
3. organize
4. arrangements
5. spare
6. presentation
7. obvious
8. achievement
9. American
10. obvious
11. organize
12. achievement
13. spare
14. research
15. arrangements
16. presentation

P. 16
1. b
2. a
3. d
4. c
5. a

P. 18
1. d
2. b
3. c
4. false
5. true
6. true
7. true
8. false

P. 20
1. a
2. c
3. b
4. c
5. d

P. 22
ACROSS
2. donated
7. fivehundredninetysix
8. assistance
DOWN
1. contributions
3. fiftyseven
4. generous
5. hesitant
6. replenish

P. 24
1. d
2. c
3. b
4. b
5. d

P. 26
1. c
2. a
3. d
4. a
5. b

P. 28
Sentences using the following words:
1. faithfully
2. longingly
3. suggestion
4. finance
5. unable
Label skis, snowmobiles, and equipment correctly.

P. 30
1. c
2. b
3. c
4. a
5. d

P. 32
1. educational
2. confident
3. dismayed
4. bashful
5. culture
6. acquainted
7. true
8. true
9. false
10. false
11. true
12. false

P. 34
1. a
2. c
3. b
4. d
5. c

P. 36
ACROSS
3. recommended
4. astronauts
5. adapt
8. imitate
DOWN
1. effects
2. separation
6. gravity
7. zeroG

P. 38
1. c
2. a
3. c
4. b
5. d

P. 40
1. d
2. a
3. c
4. c
5. b

P. 42
ACROSS
3. relatives
4. communication
7. support
8. grandparents
DOWN
1. opportunities
2. advances
5. generations
6. advantages

P. 44
1. b
2. d
3. a
4. c
5. d

P. 46
Sentences using the following words:
1. assured
2. gigantic
3. fraction
4. purchased
5. overwhelmed
6. exhibits
7. artistic
8. conclusion

P. 48
1. b
2. c
3. a
4. d
5. c

P. 50
1. assignment
2. keen
3. arrangement
4. fumes
5. debate
6. behavior
7. illness
8. discussions
9. fact
10. opinion
11. opinion
12. fact
13. fact

P. 52
1. b
2. c
3. d
4. a
5. c

P. 54
1. a
2. c
3. d
4. b
5. b

P. 56
1. attitude
2. curiosity
3. clambered
4. apologize
5. true
6. false
7. true
8. true
9. false
10. true

P. 58
1. a
2. c
3. d
4. a
5. c

P. 60
Sentences using the
following words:
1. unbroken
2. unkempt
3. apparent
4. speechless
5. referred
6. comments
7. overgrown
8. charming

P. 62
1. c
2. a
3. d
4. b
5. c

P. 64
ACROSS
1. wafting
3. pronounced
6. delightful
7. entangled
DOWN
2. aroma
3. pasture
4. occurred
5. heavenly

P. 66
1. b
2. a
3. c
4. d
5. a

P. 68
1. a
2. c
3. d
4. b
5. c

P. 70
1. risked
2. orbited
3. Unfortunately
4. survive
5. capsule
6. oxygen
7. chimp
8. recovered
9. recovered
10. orbited
11. survive
12. oxygen
13. unfortunately
14. risked
15. capsule
16. chimp

P. 72
1. b
2. d
3. a
4. d
5. c

P. 74
1. b
2. c
3. d
4. false
5. false
6. true
7. true
8. false

P. 76
1. c
2. c
3. b
4. c
5. a

P. 78
ACROSS
2. local
4. flecks
6. addition
8. certificate
DOWN
1. porcelain
3. companion
5. content
7. petite

P. 80
1. c
2. b
3. c
4. a
5. d

P. 82
1. d
2. a
3. c
4. d
5. b

P. 84
1. abandoned
2. economics
3. quarry
4. resource
5. protection
6. reserve
7. sites
8. decaying
9. opinion
10. fact
11. fact
12. fact
13. opinion

P. 86
1. c
2. a
3. c
4. d
5. c

P. 88
1. seamen
2. voyages
3. menacing
4. inhabitants
5. categories
6. squid
7. dismiss
8. prehistoric
9. true
10. false
11. true
12. false
13. true

P. 90
1. c
2. a
3. d
4. b
5. d

P. 92
ACROSS
4. rewind
6. available
7. credits
8. plot
DOWN
1. previews
2. climax
3. feature
5. detail

P. 94
1. d
2. b
3. c
4. a
5. c